out crept the stars

a collection

by Anthony G. Cirilla

To: Zach, Fellow Lit Geek, Comrade in Hating Gaiman's ClozI Beowulf, Associate of Bottle Room Conferences

From: Anthony G. Cirilla

PUBLISH AMERICA

PublishAmerica
Baltimore

ISBN: 1-60836-319-8
PUBLISHED BY PUBLISHAMERICA, LLLP
www.publishamerica.com
Baltimore

Printed in the United States of America

Dedication

This collection is dedicated to my grandmother,
Patricia Cirilla,
for her constant support of my writing
and her angelic presence in my life.

Acknowledgements

Special thanks to Dr. Martin for his continual support and editorial advice.
Thanks to Mom, Jason, John and everyone else who had faith in me.
Thank you, Jesus Christ, for giving me a chance to write my words.
And thank you, reader, for giving me a chance to be heard.

Foreword

Briefly, I would like to discuss with you what I have attempted in the following pages. There is here a combination of poems and short stories which dwell upon a great variety of themes. Included are the powers of the imagination, the value of free will, the importance of critical thinking, and the necessity of keeping an open mind to the spiritual world, to name a few. I wanted to experiment in a different art form. Unfortunately, my talent is giving to rambling, which is why I had initially chosen the form of the novel. One may assume that short stories and poems are easier than novels because they are shorter. In some cases, that can be true, but generally such an assumption is erroneous. Writing shortly and succinctly is difficult, as any college student well knows, and a mediocre writer may take several hundred pages to do what a poet or short story writer can do better in a few lines. So I have tried to broaden my horizons, as the saying goes, and work in forms of media which are outside of my comfort zone.

Allow me, if you will, to make a few comments about poetry in specific, as I feel it is perhaps the most important break from my usual inclinations in terms of my own writing endeavors. Poetry is, I think, the hardest thing to write. Of course, it is easy to pick up a pen and scurry it across the page, come up with some awkward stanzas and *call* the thing you just wrote a poem. What I mean, certainly, is that it is hard to write poems well. The art harbors challenges no other writer faces. Make no mistake; novels, short stories, and even non-fiction present many difficulties. But the hardship the poet faces is uniquely linguistic, and I think peculiar to his efforts.

The problem, really, is between style and from, verses freedom and creativity. Traditions of poetry abound in anthologies, and within those traditions each good poet at times reaffirms certain aspects and rejects others. Poets are in that way much like profound religious thinkers. When their art is deemed passé or unnecessary by critics, they shake their heads sadly and think,

7

"You don't know what you're missing."

Poetry, like religion, calls for both text and testing. As Scripture gives structure and the heart gives that structure life, so does the poet immerse himself in his poetic community, dialoguing with kindred and disonate voices from the past. Poetry is not merely a *this*; it is not simply a noun. Poetry is largely a verb. It has been done, behaved, affirmed, and argued. It is the grounds of philosophy, spirituality, morality. There is no subject left untouched or unexplored by poetry; there is nothing a poem cannot do or say.

But this freedom comes at a cost. Because poetry is the language of those who care, cynics shrink from it and say it is too easy. Young poets embrace the freedom it offers, but they forget the gravity that must accompany even the most lighthearted of poems. It is a struggle to write something that entertains, uplifts, and distracts, while talking smartly, deeply, and usefully. Poetry is the highest science; it is the science of humanity, and it is no wonder that such a science would be so difficult to pull off.

I do not claim to achieve this poetic majesty. Far from it. I will readily call myself a novelist or a writer. Not necessarily a good one, but I will take the title. But Poet, well. That is a title of profound responsibility, and no one should take it lightly. Attempted here, then, are poems not by a poet, but an experimenter. They are toys, and some of them are broken and a little worn. But I hope to share with their readers a love of language, a love of thought, and a love of the poetic spirit.

My work, both in poetry and prose, is highly influenced by William Blake and the other Romantics, as well as Dante, Homer and the Bible writers, among others. Not everyone can sit in such high company as theirs, I know. But it seems to me that no life should be lived without ever writing a poem, and certainly I feel that everyone should read poetry and poetic expression (which short stories often are). It is a sacred language, and the holy should be embraced and entertained in our midst with the honor it deserves. So come, sit, and talk with me for a while.

Paradiso

"…it has come as auxiliary to another favorite Speculation of mine, that we shall enjoy ourselves here after by having what we calle happiness on Earth repeated in a finer tone and so repeated—And yet such a fate can only befall those who delight in sensation rather than hunger as you do after Truth…"
—John Keats

You already know the story I am going to tell you. You have heard this a million times before. In fact, this whole thing may have nothing new or useful for you at all. But it is all I know, all I have to say, and I do not demand that you listen to me. I am simply going to tell you what the truth is. You may not want to hear it, which is fine. But stay with me if you are brave. Try to stop hiding from the pain of what you know, or nothing here will mean anything to you.

Our planet is called Paradiso, as it has for some years. After the mantra of Nietzsche grew popular, the star-ward gaze was abandoned and we got to calling earth heaven. Science so holy has salvaged our world, welded it like an impregnable casket. Huge bridges, like the cables of a hunting spider's web, have joined the continents, and Pangea is an apt name of the world-wide nation.

There is no hunger on Paradiso. The machines have pumped the life from the soil, and every human mouth is fed. There is no labor but luxury, for pursuits of the mind are the commandment of Pangea. Everyone is stylized a scholar, and violence is strictly and rigorously forbidden. There are no wars between factions, because Pangea says that every person is equally unique, and all individuality is carefully apportioned by the officials. The differences of the old world, we are taught, only cause pain, so we are relieved of dangerous heritage.

Disease is a fairytale on Paradiso, a story told by the historians we call doctors. Medicine is kept in museums once known as hospitals. Life is longer now, and they say immortality will be on the market any day. The harder we work, the longer we are allowed to live, and Pangea is praised as a perfect government for how well we run its stipulations.

They call the old world Inferno in the texts. A horrible place where people can't agree on the simplest beliefs and blood is spilt over things that matter. Now we can be happy, free of their fanaticism. We no longer have to worry about truth. We have our manufactured happiness, and they assure us that it is enough.

It is true that we are happy. No one dies untimely, and everyone pursues what they are supposed to want. They, we, are blissful, as only ignorance can allow.

I am called Faustus. I would have introduced myself earlier, but this is not a story about me. It is a story about us, and the Pangean Paradise. You know, we are a peaceful people. Really, far more peaceful than the old world. The citizens of the disunified Inferno would have been jealous at our widespread, global, organized machine of perfect utility. Pleasure is for nearly every human in Paradiso all that is known; there are no smiles tinted by sadness.

There is a secret to Paradiso's success. You know it, I know you do. But you forgot it. Understandable. You were busy living your life, and it couldn't be helped anyway. I will remind you.

At birth, I was assigned the task of Deliverer. There is a class on Paradiso known as the Champions. The highest of Champions, most honored, are the Heroes. They are the heartbeat, the source, of Pangea's culture machine. Then there are the Attendants. Finally, there is my class. The Deliverers, we live between. We see and live in two worlds. We see the peace of Paradiso, and we see the small microcosm, the world entirely created by Pangea: Purgatorio. That is the realm of the Heroes.

I will familiarize you again with what certainly merely slipped from your mind. As the Deliverer, I watch every child born into my assigned district. I mark them silently, and according to the criteria, carefully discern who are to be Heroes. I write this down in my personal files, and meet the parents clandestinely. I inform them, and console them of the honor Pangea proscribes.

At the proper age, I take the child from their parents. The Hero is taken at its first lie. Usually in Paradiso this is not until very old, for humans are raised to strict codes of behavior. But Heroes are different. Lying is in their genes.

I remember my first Hero. Her lie was reported on a cool Monday morning—not too cool, for weather is carefully supervised—and I apprehended her at seven thirty a.m. Her lie was that she enjoyed waking early. Her personal diary, recorded orally, testified that early mornings made her unhappy. I took her from her parents at eight fifteen a.m. She was three and a half years old.

I took her to the Attendants. She held her storybook close, scared but brave. Her parents had told her they were proud of her. Their ashen faces told her that they were scared. I felt proud for her fortitude. I know why she is a Hero.

For six months she was prepared in Purgatorio. I am not an Attendant, so I had nothing more to do with her. Pangean code suggests Deliverers watch little or nothing of the process. After that first time, I seldom ever watched.

The child is fed sparingly over those six months and put through extensive exercise. Heroes are expected to be in excellent physical condition. She was no different. At the end of the sixth month she was taken from the outer hall of the Purgatorio, to where the final steps are taken inside.

The child is stripped. All hair is removed, down to each eyelash. Then a careful process removes the thinnest layer of skin across the entire body. This heightens the sensitivity. The instruments are brought out, and the attendant sets to work. The child is given something to bite on.

Usually the damage to the internal organs and the shock of pain kills the Hero within an hour. The process is necessary. It is the only way to generate enough innocent pain. The scientists tap into the karma program, and for many years enough pain is generated, and enough energy, to produce relief across Pangea. Paradiso is a land of utter pleasure, thanks to the efforts of our noble Heroes. The machine runs on blood, just a little is enough, every once in a while.

You start, upset. Look, you say, at all the lives this makes better. This process causes planet-wide healing, you insist. Surely, it is reasonable to make the entire world for this occasional, routine sacrifice.

Certainly. Reasonable.

In Between

My shoes were cold
from lying on the garage floor.
It was dark; there was just enough
light to open the door.

I stepped from the still cold
and into the night wind,
the garbage can towed behind me.
I barely lifted my gaze most of the way.

Then I turned, and looked up, and saw
the stars, sparkling like the sprinkling of snow
dotted across the yard. And I thought their
glow was proper for poetry.

But then I thought, everyone gazes at the
stars and thinks about their beauty.
But they miss the real awe,
the place in-between that allows the stars to shine.

It is the biggest place in the sky,
but is seen the least
because it does not sparkle.

Freedom

When the wise man rules, the city falls. No fools abide by his ways.
Good kings are ignored and forgotten, trampled by the endless progression
of heedless time.
I stood and waited, but the demon would not speak. I listened and hoped
for guidance, but my pen went unmoved. The daughters of Zeus may be
too fickle to love or trust.
Forging forever the wordsmith finds chaos; relax your grip and the flow
will come. Organization is natural; tyranny will never bring order to words.
I do not seek to mean, only to say. It is not my purpose to get to your point,
so don't expect any different.
So here we are with no purpose in mind. Recline with me a while and
forget your agendas. Do not look always for intrigue and plot and a thou-
sand other subtleties unnecessary to the art. They will come in time. Simply
wait; patiently enjoy the rhythm of what you hear. Where you go is not so
grand a question as how.
Drift this way for moments, if you can, and see where you find your-
self. Not every body of water is a rapid river or surging ocean, tumultuous
and fierce and windswept and driven. Just wait and let the air fill your
lungs, and observe the lake at calm. Enjoy the quiet and relish that which
has no form. Structure alone has no power. In freedom beats the heart of
the masterpiece; there you will find it.
Do not rush me or demand my aims. If I were shooting arrows I had
better aim well, but these things I write are not weapons. They are balloons
held in tiny fists, released and carried and off wherever. Do not fight the
wind or try to tame it. Wind is for dancing, not discipline.
"What is the wise man for?" you ask.
To guide, never to rule. Listen to his words and know them, but do not
focus too hard, or you will forget to dance.

The Wizard

Immortality is inscribed in the hearts of men.

Screaming under the stars of Aries, he was born in the highlands. Raised by soft hands, shown the secret scrolls of life by those who themselves did not fully comprehend their value, he learned. They gave him access to knowledge, and they gave him what his body needed, but they did not give him his name.

No, it was in the tomes he found the name, and from his teachers he knew it. From those secret mentors he was christened the Wizard. In his youth he blossomed, growing greater and greater in wisdom, learning and perceiving reality to depths that those many years older than him would never attain.

As is inevitable with wisdom, the Wizard, as he studied, learned a most devastating truth. He was going to die. It might be the next day, or in many years, but it would happen, despite the powers he possessed, for it happened to all, both common men and even to wizards that had gone before.

Terrified, the wizard told himself, "I will not perish like an ordinary man," though he himself was yet a boy. So, he turned to his secret teachers, to the voices of the parent wizards that gave him his power.

For months he was closed from reality, from family and friends, and in that time, a grave chasm was wrought. Those close to him became unfamiliar, those who once knew him thought him alien now, and those who might know him were too unsure to try. And as this chasm grew, the Wizard was driven more to the scrolls and to the hidden teachers, and he began to create wizardry of his own in new, wondrous inventions. Yet he did not share them, but kept them, jealous of their value and afraid of scorn from a world that would not understand his achievements.

Yet, all of his experiments with wizardry, astounding as many of them were, could not yield one thing: eternal life. Elixirs, concoctions, decanters of all sort, with scribbling denoting their use and purpose, populated his underground lair beside the scrolls. Any one of his creations would well have rendered even his superiors awestruck, but the Wizard was overcome by his personal desire, unable to see now that he was powerful at all, and had come to think of himself as a failure and as worthless for not attaining the unattainable.

Darkness came over the Wizard, over his soul, yet in his craft he remained bound, unable to, at any waking moment, put it out of mind.

Then, one fateful night, his wizardry went awry. He survived, though he was damaged, and he knew then that his attempts to stop death had killed him, and soon he would be no more. With what time he had left, the Wizard destroyed much of his failed work, especially what was dangerous of it, and decided to leave in better hands what was left, if any of it should be of value. So he turned to the gentle hands that had brought him to this world, and he revealed to them his creations.

In the moment that they realized the depths of his genius, the Wizard died.

"His power was great, and we never saw," they sighed.

"What did he do to ruin himself? It is such a tragedy..."

"I know not, but his works will change the world, if the world will see it."

"Yes. He is gone, but his triumphs will endure."

Saddened, they buried him, and when others learned the greatness of the Wizard, they too were sad, and wished they had known him while he yet lived, and wished he had not fallen to such a dark fate, that his power might have blessed the world further. But their wishes were too late.

Alas, the lonesome Wizard would never know that he was immortal.

An Absolute Personal Myth

The names come first.
Draw the widest shapes, then the smaller ones
and use a pencil.
Then erase everything.
And color inside where you remember
the lines used to be.

Gods and geniuses make distinctions
evil men make distinctions separate
and creators walk a line
between uniformity
    anarchy
        hatred
            rebellion
                brainwashing.
Satan cries for in the bloody Styx
he washes his slaves
and wants their love but you can't love
if you're not a god.

In the beginning
Guilt created the gentlemen and the jury
and gave up divinity for raging
tyrannical idols of earth, flesh
and tombstones.

In a beginning somewhere,
someone got it right
then started over
to make things more interesting.

Lamentation

Nothing is everywhere
and the world spins
with a vicious mercy.

Dragons hide in their caves
as landscapers stroll by
and mermaids weakly swim,
choking on the pollution
of poisoned minds and dead
imaginations.

The witch's chant was broken,
distracted by the bored reporter
droning on about the apocalypse.

In a corner of empty Mount Olympus,
I sat and began to weep.

The Tro Breizh

Ivo Kemtin stood impatiently at the bus corner, glancing at his watch every few moments. He had to be to work soon, and he'd missed the last bus by literally ten seconds. He had watched it, unbelieving, as it pulled away into the rush of traffic, like a whale merging amongst a school of angry minnows. Now he was going to be late, there was no doubt about it, but if the next bus came a few minutes early, there was a chance he might make it within the seven-minute leeway. He could hear his boss's voice, the same rant bout responsibility and what-not...

Sighing, Ivo sat down and pulled out a huge volume from his work bag. Might as well read for a few minutes while he waited. He opened the book to page 230 and started reading. He never bookmarked or dog-eared; Ivo lost his bookmarks and hated to damage his books. It was just easier to stop at the end of a chapter or on an even page and remember it from there.

The squeal and hiss of the bus's tires broke Ivo's concentration, and noting the page number he slammed the book shut and stuffed it in his bag while bolting into the door. He dropped a few coins into the bus slot and nodded to the driver with a smile, then looked for a seat. It wasn't difficult; for some reason most of the seats were empty. That seemed unusual, considering the time of day. Ivo shrugged and seated himself on a cold, plastic blue chair and leaned against the metallic wall of the bus. As the door closed and the vehicle merged with traffic, a light rain started to patter outside. Just in time. Ivo was glad he didn't get caught in that.

He still had a good twenty-five minute ride. After a few minutes of zoning and thinking about his girl—ex-girlfriend—for some strange reason, he decided he might as well read a little more.

The bus stopped before Ivo got anywhere. That jarred him. He looked up, and gazed out the window. He couldn't see anything. The window was lined with a heavy, roiling fog that kept visibility to almost nothing. *I don't remember there being a stop this soon...*

A man in a thick raincoat boarded the bus. He walked slowly, looking up and down the aisles as though he were making a vastly important choice. Then he walked over to Ivo and gave him a crinkly, nice old-man smile.

"Hello, lad."

"Hello, sir," nodded Ivo absently.

The man sat next to him. Ivo thought that was a little strange. The bus was almost entirely empty. Why...

"You know, my stop is soon. You will have to get up. Did you want to sit across the way?"

"Oh, no. I'd like some company, if that's all right. I'll move for you, when your time comes."

Ivo shrugged. No reason to be rude, he supposed. "Okay."

There was a minute or two of silence, except for the steady noise of the bus doing its job. Then, the driver spoke.

"A little radio, aye, lad?"

Ivo realized the question was aimed at him, somehow. The Scottish accent he detected startled him. But then, this was NYC. All sorts of people ended up in NYC. "Well, sure."

It was a talk show. Someone was talking about the ugly campaign.

"Really, I don't think religion has got anything to do with it. I want a leader who can..."

He was rudely interrupted by a strong feminine voice. "How can you possibly say that? Most of the country..."

The driver switched it immediately, and a chorus of instrumentals hummed behind a strong, Italian basso singer.

"Ah, such a pity, ain' it, to be hearing such things?" mused the old man.

"What, crooners?" joked Ivo.

The man smiled. "Nae, not crooners. It's fussin' over religion an' sich, that I'm sayin'."

"Well, what can you expect? Religion causes problems. It always has."

The old man looked sad at that comment. "Has it, now?"

"Sure. Look at the world. Look at history. America wouldn't be here if it weren't for the problems religion causes."

"Aye, aye it wouldn'. I expect many people wouldn't be here, if it weren't for those problems."

Ivo looked at him. "Are you religious?"

"Well, ye know, now. Everyone's religious."

"Not everyone."

"Oh, aye? That so?"

"It is."

"Like who?"

"Well, atheists."

"Is that what you are?" There was no accusation or hostility in the question, but for some reason it still made Ivo uncomfortable.

"No, not really. I mean, I'm not sure."

"Not sure? Not sure if you're an atheist?

"No. I'm not sure what I am at all."

The old man smiled. "And atheists aren't religious?"

"No." Ivo shrugged. "I mean, they don't believe in God, right?"

"Indeed, that's what the word is meaning," chuckled the old man. Ivo turned red at his own foolish comment. "Does an atheist eat?"

"Of course."

"Well, why?"

"Because he doesn't want to be hungry?"

"And why should that be?"

"Because, um, no one wants to be hungry?"

"True enough, mostly. So don't he then behave for that reason, then?"

"Yeah, I guess."

"And should you smack an atheist a good one, won't he have a feeling towards ye for it?"

"Of course, he will."

"So you have a man who has a belief about God, and about how he should act about certain feelings, and that he shouldnae care for certain kinds of actions. It's no congregation he's started, but that's a religion all the same, lad."

Ivo hadn't thought of that. "Yeah, I suppose. What does all that get you?"

"Well, I dinnae know, lad, I dinnae, but what does it get ye?"

The bus stopped, interrupting their conversation. Ivo checked his timepiece. This had to be him. He looked out the window, then balked. The mist had rolled away, revealing a wet, grassy countryside, an empty field with not a building in sight. What…

"What is this? Is this some kind of joke?" He stood and moved past the old man, then strolled to the door. Or where the door should have been. But it was

20

gone. He turned to the driver, who was wearing a kilt.

"I, what… Wait. I'm dreaming, right?"

"Dreaming? Lad, ye dream every day at work, ye dream every day at school. Ye dream all the morning away and ye dream all the night to dust. Ye want to wake, ye do, and most don't these days. We find the ones who want to wake, and we bring them along for a little while. Life is a long sleep, and it is a fitful one, and the hardest things are the least real and the softest things the most. I tell ye, if ye think ye're dreaming then it's the best chance at waking ye can have in this world."

Ivo blinked. His mind reeled with confusion. He just wanted to go to work, and have a boring day, and come home and go to bed. "What's the deal here?"

"Well, ye have seven trials if ye find yer way to this here bus."

"Why seven?"

The driver paused, and he looked confused himself for a minute. He turned and looked at the old man, but had to look back out at the medieval-looking road to keep driving.

"Hey, Pol, now have at it? Why *do* we make it seven?"

"Well, what's wrong with seven?"

"Nothing, I suppose. Though I nae ken it myself, and it's a wee bit odd."

"Aye. Seven, and there's a reason to it, laddie. But knowing why you're here won't get you off the bus. Knowing why you're anywhere is a lot less important than a lot of other questions, you know."

Ivo sighed and sat down. For some reason, he felt rather calm about this whole thing. Though logic seemed to have fled the scene, there was a strange familiarity to these men. And rather than make a fuss, he supposed it best to go along with it. After all, there was something odd about them, and he didn't want to make any enemies. It was his nature to go with the flow, if it avoided unnecessary conflict.

"So, what are these trials, then?"

"Ah, aye, now that's a better question," smiled the old man. Ivo turned to look at him, feeling the vibrations in the back of his chair. "Well, you've passed three already."

Ivo raised an eyebrow. "Three?"

"Oh, aye, three."

"I didn't notice."

"Well, of course not. You're not supposed to notice everything. That's part

21

of the game. If you notice everything too soon, you might as well not play. The surprises are what learn you something, lad."

"So what were they?"

"Well, now. The first was to get on the bus. If ye dinnae do that, laddie, there'd be nothing to say and we couldn' do nothing for ye," said the driver.

"But I didn't know…"

"Of course ye didn't. We jes' said ye wouldn'! And that's just the point, for certain. The bus could have taken ye right to work, sure, but ye couldnae known that totally. And ye got on the right way, ye did."

"What made it the right way?"

"Well, it's a little complicated," said the old man. "The second test was letting me sit next to you. If you hadn't done that, you might never have gotten off the bus."

"I still haven't."

The old man smiled. "Aye."

"And the third?"

The driver laughed. "The third, laddie, the third was bound either way, with ye. Ye asked a good question."

Ivo thought back, but for some reason the conversation was becoming muddled in his poor, tiring brain. These past few moments had been the strangest of his entire life. "Which question was it?"

"Well, the best of the ones ye asked. A few were fine, but the one, why, that was a gem, it was." The bus lurched as the driver pressed the break. "Aye, an' here we are, true."

"Where are we?"

"Laddie, ye look mighty tired. Sit back and wait a spell."

Ivo sat up suddenly. "Did you say my name?"

"Aye. I said, up with ye, Ivo."

"But how'd ye—er, you know my name?"

The driver grinned. "Why, I'm knowing every name of every man what steps on my bus, laddie." He adjusted his kilt absently. "Besides, if ye think hard enough on it, ye ken mine too."

Ivo made an incredulous expression, then realized with a start that he *did* know the man's name. "Duns Scotus. Wait. I know that name. But he's been dead for…hundreds of years."

"Aye. Except on this bus. I come back to drive. Least I can do. And that old laddie back there, ye're knowin' his name, I'm sure of it."

"You shouldn't be speaking English," muttered Ivo.

"Aye, and who said I was? Ye hear what ye might ken on this bus, laddie."

"He's Pol Aurelian. He was made a saint of the Church, same as you were made a doctor of it."

"And how are ye knowing that, laddie?"

"I dinnae-don't know."

The driver grinned. "Ye always know yer own on this bus, I tell ye. Good laddie. Take a look out there, tell me what ye see."

Ivo complied. Outside the window he could see a Scottish family at work in the yard. They wore ancient clothing, but all authentic. One man stopped working, and looked up and waved. Ivo waved back. The scene moved along the farmlands until they came to a school. A man wearing teacher's clothing walked towards the bus.

Ivo turned, and the man was sitting next to him. "Hello, Ivo."

"Hello, Tobias Smollet."

"Take these, and write me a letter when you get to your desk at work."

"But you'll be dead, outside of the bus," said Ivo, somehow knowing it.

Tobias smiled. "That's true. I will be dead. But you see, letters, they are for all people. If you write a word, you don't just write it for you or for the readers. That word is the same word used since the first chapter, and the same word that will be used at the last page. I'll never read your letter, but I've read your words, so you have to write it if you want to keep all of us alive."

Ivo wasn't sure, but he thought he was beginning to understand. At that moment, Tobias Smollet was gone. The bus lurched, and they stopped in front of his work.

"Do ye know what yer tests were, laddie?"

"Aye," said Ivo.

"And, did you learn something from it?" asked Pol.

"I think I will, once I get to my desk," said Ivo.

"Good lad," the driver and the other passenger said together.

Ivo got off the bus, and turned and looked to see that the driver was a black man wearing ordinary, NYC clothes. The bus was packed full of people eager to get to their destinations. Ivo nodded to the man, who nodded back politely. The door closed, and the big vehicle merged with traffic.

Turning to the building, Ivo looked at his watch. He was ten minutes early.

Shrugging, he went inside, clocked in, and went to his desk. A quill and a curled piece of parchment was waiting for him, next to his computer keyboard.

"Hey, Ivo," said his boss. "How was your ride in?"

"It woke me up a little."

Goodbye, but Never Goodbye

Oh, to touch her hand again.
To see her smile.
To kiss her gray head.
Simple things I felt I'd always have
Though I knew better
And when the better got the best of me
Shattering hearts, there's no stopping the tears.

Half a decade short of a century
A life lived so full, so real
So true, so warm.
Wrinkled hands, smile ever ready,
Eyes twinkling with affection,
"You eat half, I eat half."
Her half was always suspiciously smaller.

I sat on her couch that night
And held a can of her Lemon-Lime soda
And soul-blood on my face
I wondered where she was
Where she went
Her heart, where, please
Please, open your eyes for me
One last time…

Love is the seed of sorrow,
Life is a trail of tears,
Tracing the lines from smile to grimace,
There are no words to say what I need to say

No voice to speak this precious pain.
I said goodbye.
But I will never say goodbye.

We hold you tight as we let you go.
And the less we have you
The more we know
We'll always have you.
Inescapable clichés,
But not they or any cute phrase
Can ever really say
Who you are or what you were.

You were Ma.
You were GRAMMA!
You were grandma downstairs.
Goodbye, but never goodbye.

Reunion

When you stop to look at the brightness
of the moon on a clear night
as it shines so radiant among the stars,
do you not wonder, as I do, who else
gazes upon its lovely face?

Perhaps on that dark night when
the light of the moon illuminates the dreaming earth
all the world stops to look with you.

In those moments the circle of the earth
moves with the circle of the heavens,
and all creation moves by the love
of a single hand.

Maybe there in the stars that one
you love waits for you,
but until then
on a clear night look at the moon
with him, and know that
you two still are one.

The Moon's Eye

"What the imagination seizes as Beauty must be truth—whether it existed before or not."
—John Keats

In ancient times, there was a fair kingdom known as Ilystra. Here dwelt noble moon elves, and in this age, theirs was a mighty kingdom, full of magical wonders as the elven folk are wont. Silver haired, tall and mighty, with piercing eyes of gray or blue, these winged folk of the moon, in this place, had reached their height in prowess. This magnificent nation flourished for many years, assessing affluence and growing ever more glorious. And there is one legend of theirs which would in later times be retold in many ways by the bards of men, and the words and names have changed, yet truth wears many faces. As it was first told to me, this is the tale.

Now, to the east was a smaller, yet mighty still, kingdom known as Broghein, ruled by the witch demon Sangohmara. She was a powerful and beautiful sorceress, known for her wretchedness and love for evil and destruction. Hers was a kingdom of goblins and orcs, and she ruled over them with an iron clad fist, using her dark powers and demon thralls to control them utterly.

The Queen of Broghein was greedy and hungry for power. She knew well of the hoard of wealth and magical strength hidden away in the vaults of Ilystra. Regardless, her black heart burned with hatred for all things Faerie, even as do all demon spawn, and no such beings did she loathe against more than the moon elves, with their regal fairness.

So, the witch demon contrived to make war upon Ilystra. Calling her goblin kin armies and demon thralls, the sorceress prepared for war. Then, on the

Hatuia festival, the most holy of elven celebrations, she attacked.

Now, to the Ilystrians the arts of war were no mystery. Indeed, these very kingdoms had before come to blows, and had no love for either one in any way. For many long years, the war would continue. Both collective warriors had no small store of power, and the fighting was extravagant far beyond the meager sorcery and war machinations of humans today.

In the heartlands of Ilystra, there was a sacred place called Ilnumin. It was a small plateau, crowned by low mountains, full of faerie magic and adorned with statues of living stone.

The princess of Ilystra, who was called Lirenna, often came to this hallowed ground, and danced by the light of the moon. Lirenna had long, silver hair and pale white skin as her people were prone. Yet her eyes were pools of fiery gold, a great rarity among her kindred. These eyes glowed in elven mystery with the light of the stars. Her beauty was perfect, and her heart was pure. The youngest of her king's daughters, Lirenna danced with a grace rare even among the most elegant of her kindred. In her hands she held a white lute crafted of elven metals, upon which she played ancient and beautiful melodies passed down by royalties of the elven folk even as she danced.

The witch demon knew of such an elven sacred place, though she knew not where it lay. So, she sent her spies and trackers forth, that she may despoil things holy to her enemies.

One among these trackers was Delthor, a hobgoblin. He was considered strange among the goblin kin, always in control of his anger, slow to become violent, and quick to bestow forgiveness. He knew little outside the witch demon's kingdom, but was not satisfied with the brutish ways of his kind, though it was a disquiet he himself did not recognize. A quiet spirit among chaos, he was never quite fulfilled. All this hid behind a gruesome, fierce visage that was considered ugly even by the standards of his hideous people.

Patiently, obedient to his mistress, Delthor searched out this holy place. For weeks, he wandered and observed, looking for clues that few would notice even if searching with the utmost care. Then, one night, when the moon was in full wax, Delthor heard a lilting voice somewhere night. So, he followed the singing, and coming upon its source, he knew that he had found the sacred land of the Ilystrians.

Yet, this was not what concerned him. Accustomed to the rough and savage ways of his kinfolk, the only beauty, and this corrupted by the vilest of evils, that he had ever beheld was the witch demon, and to the elven princess he now witnessed, she did not compare.

Hiding carefully, Delthor watched this descendant of faerie as she moved and played her lute, and stopped to sing, then continued on the lute. Faerie magic shimmered about her, yet the stronger spell she cast was less of magic and more borne out of simple grace and gentleness, silvery wings flowing about her.

Delthor was breath taken. In that moment, he wanted even less of anything to do with his people than ever before. Delthor was filled with a yearning, a hunger to be other than what he was. To be elven.

Then, the hobgoblin saw a dark form rising nearby, seeking to close in upon in secrecy the princess. He knew it for it was; another tracker, and worse yet, an orc, full of unclean strength and wrath.

Lirenna's eyes met with Delthor's for an instant. He didn't know she'd noticed him, but he knew she didn't see the other, less obvious danger. Regardless of what she knew, Lirenna continued to dance.

As the orc prepared his battleaxe to strike, Delthor propelled himself from his hiding place, and intercepted his kin.

"Brother, for what do you assail me?" he demanded.

Delthor did not answer. They battled fiercely in the crisp night, and the orc dropped to the earth, lifeless.

Lirenna had stopped dancing, and watched him. "Of a strange sort is one of the goblin kin, on the first account for watching with gentle interest and joy the dance of an elf. Then, it would be considered twofold as odd, for one such as thee, to actually face down thy own kindred for the sake of a very enemy to thy kingdom. What would one such as this desire?"

Delthor was not sure how to respond. He thought, and then said, "I wish for a better way."

She smiled. "Yes, surely, that is a wish of my people as well as many others. Always some bleak thing stands between our true desires. It be true, indeed, that I've no care in my heart for yon kindred; the goblin kin art in no ways noble, far as I have yet to know."

"I hold this in no way against thee, for mine people art the wickedest and most savage of all things vile. Living thus among them, think I that I've much less love in my heart for them than even thee."

So, the beautiful princess and ugly hobgoblin spoke into the hour of dawn, and separated as great friends. Delthor continued to visit her, even dispatching further other goblin kin that happened upon the sacred Ilnumin, and soon they met there every night. It was not long erstwhile Lirenna's beauty and gracious manner caused Delthor to fall in love with her, and only a little time before her keen perception pierced his race and outwardly unsightly appearance, to discover his gentle soul, and become equally enamored.

Both began to be noticed in their absence. The king of Ilystra was not worried for his daughter, knowing her magic's to be well fit as protection. Yet her strange disappearances, once only every full moon, had grown to be every night. Slowly, he became suspicious, and decided that she was either in harm's way or up to some mischief of sorts. So, he decided to follow her one night, and see what she was about.

The witch demon had also come to note the cyclic disappearances of one of her own. Delthor moved mysteriously from her vision every night, and now and then, others would leave to never return. Needing the tracking skills that he had, Sangohmara decided to follow him and watch what he did while gone from moonrise to moonset.

Both elven king and witch demon were following their own, when they met by chance. Enemies to the fullest, they began to fight from the first instant.

Finally the king roared, "Cease, dog of sorcery! I have pressing business. Let me tend it, and then we shall finish this."

The witch demon replied, "Very well. I've my own quest; we can wait to settle our differences."

The king, beginning to grow in suspicion of their chanced meeting, said, "Why doth thee sneak about so? Look thee for someone?"

"Indeed, for one of mine own named Delthor hast been going off hither, where I know not, for long whiles. I contrive to find out what foolishness it is that he is now a part of."

The king nodded. "So much as I thought. Then it is true. Mine own daughter hath been slipping off from dusk 'til dawn, up to some plot or thing I know nothing of. Perhaps, thy very Delthor hath been meeting with my daughter. Mayhap thy servant is traitorous towards thee!"

The witch demon grew quickly livid. "Nay, fool! It is thy brat child that is treacherous against thee!"

The king also became angry, and would normally have attacked in fury there, but shook his head and replied, "No. We can bicker like foolish children, or we can discover the truth behind Princess Lirenna and Delthor. I care not whatever thy choice may be, yet the latter is mine."

She conceded, although not without apprehension. "Very well. Let us go."

And so, they separated, each following their own. So it was that all four met at last, in the hallowed ground of Ilystra, that very Ilnumin.

Delthor and Lirenna were thunderstruck as mistress and father appeared, following close behind. The king's wrath burned almost as hot as the witch demon's.

He roared, "Lirenna, what fool thing doth thee do?" as the evil Queen roared something similar to Delthor.

The hobgoblin said, "Please, be not wrathful. Be at ease, for I have brought no harm to this fair elven princess, nor hath I done any sort of treachery against thee, my fair mistress. All that hath gone hither is Lirenna and I did grow to be friends."

Lirenna said, "Indeed, we hath no dark interests, only simple friendship, just as he does proclaim."

The king scoffed. "What now, you make friends with slugs and rats? With filthy, wicked curs? Listen, daughter, and listen well, the people of yon hobgoblin art wretched and unclean. I will not suffer thee to be in the presence of such demonic filth!"

The witch demon turned again to the king of the moon elves in anger, but realizing her disadvantage her in the holy place of her enemies, controlled her wrath, and sent it forth rather against Delthor. "Thee art goblin kin, long past descendant of the mighty demons and servant of my greatness! I shall not allow you to tarry in the presence of these donkey eared wretches! They are foolish, goatherds, worthless pigs, and thee art their enemy! Associate not with these sour, lesser beasts!"

It was at these words that the king did lose control of his own temper. Summoning the powers at his command, he attacked the witch demon. She was not unprepared and struck back. Soon, their battle was fully underway.

Delthor shouted, "No! Do not make war any longer! Foolish pride will help none of us here. Listen to me!"

They stopped, and looked in awe and confusion at him.

"We cannot continue fighting in this wretched manner. Please, let—"

"I've enough of your accursed altruism, traitor!" screamed the witch demon.

Sangohmara called upon her powers of darkness, and she sent crackling red flames to consume his body. The king was horrified by this terrible use of magic, even upon a hobgoblin, and Lirenna cried out in anguish. As his blackened, ugly form hit the earth, she ran to him.

"No! Please, Aroslumin, help me! I beg of you, aid your faithful servant in her hour of need!"

In that instant, both the king and the witch demon realized that their powers were temporarily suspended from their calling. The girl's plea had not gone unheard. For, there in the sacred place of the moon elves, Aroslumin, moon god of those very same elves, had the authority to act. So it was, that a glorious being had appeared. His hair was silver and his clothes were white, and around him was a cloak of mighty power. He spoke thusly:

"Oh young child of mine, thee hast loved one most difficult to. Thy spirit is pure, and his is gentle, and love is blossomed irredeemably. I admire thy bravery, and his, and so take this gift, and in all your days you may be joyful. Be at peace, and walk in good spirit for many years. Farewell."

And hence, with a silvery glow of mystery, Aroslumin was gone. It could then be discerned a glowing beam, stronger than all others, falling from the moon. This thing impacted close beside Lirenna yet not to her danger, creating where it struck a small crater.

She gingerly took it, fearing lest it be hot. Yet, even despite its warmth, it was pleasing to hold. She took it, and found it to be a silver rock crafted in the very form of an eye. As if knowing innately how it was to be wielded, she lifted it to the air.

Light poured forth from it, and entwined Delthor. His body was healed, and then began to change. Rapidly, the ugliness melted away, and the form of a hobgoblin shimmered and grew to the visage of a handsome moon elven lord. So it was that Delthor rose anew, now in the form of his heart.

He smiled to Lirenna. "Thank you. You have found my better way."

The Moon's Eye, however, was not completed in its work, for it does have this power; to see into the depths of any soul wearing a guise not its own, and bring out the truth of what is borne on that being's heart. And it did see the fairness of the witch demon's countenance, but saw within her vanity and wickedness. And so came forth its purifying light once more, casting in truth Sangohmara's form. And she did become ugly to behold, so ugly that she herself was terrified of her reflection. For an ugly soul can never keep a beautiful face.

Silver wings swooping behind him as he turned on his feet possessed of a new grace, Delthor said to his former mistress, "Witch demon, you are now what you always were. Leave these holy grounds, and never return, end your war against Ilystra, and you may yet live."

She bellowed a dark spell, saying, "So, you hide behind magic?! You are still ugly, I am still beautiful! Die!"

Her magic, this time, failed before his newly acquired might. He cast her strength off, and she did grow even more terrified, and so ran off into the darkness of the night, never to make violence upon the moon elves ever again.

Delthor and Lirenna were, of course, wed, keeping the Moon's Eye as a treasured heirloom. And they lived as people of legend well should; happily ever after.

Unoriginality Unfought

Blue herrings and gulls swoop over
The rippling surface of the deep bay
And tall stand the great leafed trees,
And the wind moves and the sky glows
And amidst nature's splendor still I feel
I prefer your beauty.

Laundry-lists and metaphors poets have
Long exhausted and clichéd;
I could talk about the starry sparkle
Of your warm, lovely eyes,
Or write about the soft beauty of your skin
That I long to touch and kiss;
I might expound on how the locks of your hair
Run more precious for me
Than streams of glinting rubies or gems.

Yes, I could gush about your laughter,
How it flows like a brook and comforts
With warmth like the sun,
Or ruminate in verse how your sweet voice
In song lifts me higher than
The highest stars in heaven.

But no, better you deserve, my emerald,
Better than has been spoken and better
Than I can say, so I will not seek to be

Grand, I will not seek to be new, I will not
Seek to be original, I will only speak what
Is true.

You are forever my twin flame, and forever
Will I love you.

A Lady's Token

I keep it in my wallet, the lock
of scarlet held by a tiny
string. I take it out when I feel the
longings of remorse. The hairspray
lingers barely, but it is enough. I remember
the rest.

Green eyes run over Marquez in translation
and one hand traces fantasies of ink
while she sips hot chamomile tea.
My wish is that the little necklace
still sits on her neck. Let her smile without regret,
with hope.

I tuck the lock away, the reverie subsides,
and I listen to other songs.
I know life's tide will bring in more of
sweet and bitter, but I'll swirl the
flavors into my tea and thank God
for memories.

The Golden Lyre

The Muses refuse to help me sing his name,
but I will do my best. I heard they were
jealous of him anyway. His name may mean
darkness, though it was his father of light
who gave him that famed lyre of gold.

Caught between triumph and grief,
it was the golden lyre in his gifted
hands that made heartless gods weep
and turned seductive sirens to silence and
opened to him the horrid gates of Hades.

Deadened to love with her gone
he declined any woman's touch,
and for his disdain the Maenads punished
and tore the sad life from the bard.

I wept at the scene of his grisly wreckage,
and lifted his lyre from the listless earth
and cleaned away the olden dust
to clear the ancient crime.
His lyre shall not go unplayed.

A Little Comedy

In the middle of the morning
my eyes were plastered open,
glued to the road.
My eyes could not blink,
for Virgil berated me from
the passenger's seat on
the very first lesson.
"If you grip your girl
the way you grip the wheel,
she will die."

At last we returned home,
and I left the inferno of instruction.
The cars gone, the household empty,
the door locked.
I would have to serve penance
or through supplication find
my way inside. I could not wait;
my phone and my keys were in the house,
and I had to clock in at work soon.

So I wrestled with a rocking chair and a window,
my very own Geryon, and I
toppled majestically into the
bathroom, just managing
to avoid cracking my skull
on the holy throne.
Inside, I found my phone

blinking with a voicemail.
I opened it, pressed a
button, and heard the maternal
words:
"There's a key in the mailbox."

Sing, Virgilian Carmentis

Sworn by the Styx
To appease mortal progeny
He turns over to the impetuous
That grand procession
Of straining steeds
Of the flaring face,
And against a wiser counsel
Than what any youth would hearken,
A world is blistered by faithless
Fools, who do not listen to their
Fathers. No, most are not struck so blatantly
By Jove's very arcing, flashing sword
But so it was for he
Who drove that caravan
So far off course;
A sad ending to a firstly harmless
Odyssey.

She sang to that singer
Of tales most heavy and grim
Of a mighty riddle King,
Who by the Olympian scribes was fated,
Their *magnum opus* of what
Freud would make his sage;
A masterpiece most tragic
Of one who wanted truth
But listened not to better
Advice from the one who saw nothing

Except, of course,
What others did not.

The very tale has been spun
By that Eleusian Carmentis
Of the great folly shown by
That glorious boar-slayer's crew,
They did not observe the
Admonition of the mountain lion
When after precarious victory
They delayed to flee,
Inviting decimation upon their fellows,
Many of their number was lost
To the savage revenge of Thracian warriors.

Let us not pass over how That self-same mutinous crew
Mistrusted their glorious leader of Homeric cunning,
Ignorant of the grave dictations of
The gale king,
Opened that Aeolian bag,
Made years from a few more days' travel,
To the blind poet she sings
Of that stupid act,
Avoidable simply had they obeyed
The command of Ithaca's crafty hero;
In this way their knavish folly
Prolonged the weary-fingered work
Of that wise weaver
Who waited patiently in the storm at home, yes, an extended plight
Fashioned by men
Who did not listen.

'Do not kill of his grazing flocks,'
Seemed to me to be
Easiest to obey of all which those
Greedy sailors
Disobeyed,

And the golden-haired avenger
Struck them all fatally,
For their stomachs
Outweighed their ears,
Leaving that great schemer in
Watery isolation;
Folly, she cries, the
Folly of men who resist instruction
To their benefit.

But now turn to this one:
He was noble, a true paradigm
Of deontology manifest,
To set aside his own 'hedon count'
And to, in some strange inverted way,
Follow the path of a worthy enemy,
A once-foe of twists and turns
But who, like him,
Found his home;
Whose own abandoned comrade
He found among the sons of the sea;
This man I heard her sing of, we know his
Name, for he makes a paragon
For the patron of Octavian.

Not like the son of the sun,
Nor like the son of his victim and his betrothed,
Least of all was he like those who discarded
The sagacious words
Of that immaculate orchestrating kin
That man once of Ilion made way
From his burning shores
With his eyes set most clearly
Down the road that he must go
As was by Jove decreed,
When even in the arms of that Carthage
Queen that loved him even to the point...

The sword's edge, as so sad goes the tale,
He relinquished even passionate bondage
In favor of wisdom on a grander scale.

And look!
Those high walls rose
And made their
Name, a name never to leave the lips
Of retrospective Muse-tugged scriveners
Who remember that lofty governance
Of Octavian and those who shared
His throne;
And had not that Ilionite
Molded of castings and cut of cloth
Like men of legends, of wars and of travels,
Heeded what was told,
Such grandeur would be lost to us
And such tales of ages old
We might never have then read.

I do not pretend to advise or to lend
Something as contrite as those three sisters
Who shared one piercing eye
As doctrine in which to have faith,
Yet as one looks ever carefully
At the history made
Of Achaean conquests and Ilion's off-sprung litter,
Of immortals and men sung grand,
Louder and stronger sang
The songs of the singer
Whose Orpheic inspiration was to tell
Of how that Trojan counterpart
Of the man of twists and turns
Made history so magnificent and reaching
Centuries past the grave
By something so very simple
As listening.

The Wise Men

Once there was a village led by the three wise men. They were all old, and had come from different lands when they were young men, years ago. They did not lead with force or charisma in this village, though perhaps they had come from lands where such things were practiced. Here they guided with words, with careful consideration, and with reasoning. Often they disagreed on many things with each other, and thought very differently about many questions, though on some things they did agree.

The villagers would consult them on many issues; leaders of war, commerce, personal and public disputes, and every other manner of problem. From each wise man they often received a different answer, and it lay to the villager to listen, to think, and then to act according to which way was wisest.

Once an angry beast attacked the village at its leisure and took whatever it wanted for food. At, leader of the warriors, went to the leaders. He said to them, "Wise ones, a great monster harms our people, and it is very strong. What shall I do?"

"Give the beast what it is after and it shall leave," said one old man.

"Trap him in a pit and stab him until he dies," said another.

"Face him bravely and he will flee in fear, or fight him hard until he or you and your men die," said the final man.

"Which way is best, wise ones?"

"The one that works," said one of them.

At dug a pit and filled it with spears, then laid it over and hid it from sight. When the beast came near he taunted it, and the beast leapt. It fell into the pit, but as it went, it grabbed At, and they fell together upon the spears and both died.

"Your advice killed him," said one old man.

"No," he replied, "that was the spear."

A plague came one day to the village and many grew sick, and some died.

The apothecary Hei did not know what to do, so he went to the wise men.

"Wise men," he said, "what shall I do?"

"Do nothing," said the first, "and the sickness will kill until it itself shall die."

"Help others," said the second, "with treatments and touches, to give them hope."

"Help no one, or you will die. Hide and meet very little, to stop the plague from spreading," suggested the last.

"I do not know which way to take," said Hei.

"Then wait until you do."

Hei told the villagers that they must not gather close to one another and that they must stay in their homes as much as possible until the fury of the plague is over. He went into his home and waited. Very few villagers listened, and many became ill, and many died, though Hei did not.

"He took the wrong advice," said one wise man.

"He took the right advice to the wrong people," said another.

One day a strong young man called Ist came to them and asked, "I have two talents. I can sing and I can fight. Which shall I use to be happy?"

"Use neither to be happy; neither is the way for that," cautioned the first old man.

"Sing to be happy, fight to be glorious," said the second.

"Fight to die young and achieve many things and lose them at death, or sing to know many things and hold life forever," said the last old man.

The young man became a great warrior and fought many battles. One day while on the field, his dead enemies about him, a spear pierced his throat, but did not kill him. His beautiful voice was lost, and so his singing too. In rage he returned, and with hoarse words he accosted the wise men.

"Your advice I have taken and their ill effects I have suffered. Our village has hurt by your words, and your words alone. I shall end your wrongful power."

With his sword he killed the wise men, and as a great warrior he made himself a leader of that place. No one dared question that man. No one asked what they must do; he told them.

"We are finally free of the wise men," he said.

The villagers asked no questions.

Problem of Evil

maybe God just threw up his hands
and walked away
disgusted by your oscillations
of complaints and demands

if there is no God you probably killed him
yourself, you misogynistic, masochistic
maledicted son of anti-intellectual pride

are my words not minced enough for you?
have I not spoke clearly, or have I maybe
offended your poor, virgin ears?
poor baby

you stand there with your axe dripping atheism
and theism alike, because you killed all meaning
with a single explosion of selfish misery
the creator's corpse at your feet and you cackling like

you've accomplished something by burning bridges
and drowning babies and eating bodies
and stuffing your bank account with the rotted flesh
of angels

well done, well done indeed
the corpse dissolves and a storm comes and an earthquake shakes
and when your head is crushed in the weight of nature's fury
it doesn't matter whether God lives or not

your hatred blinds
and your axe has double blades

Thou Shall Not Doubt

The cries of the machine are
crushing your skull
with slow sadistic pressure
with a careful measure
to strip away your carnal truth.
(Don't listen to me, listen!
THOU SHALL NOT DOUBT)

The machine begins to close
thin strips of sharp metal touch your face
and press against your skin
and scrape slow against the sin
of a whole body.
(Don't listen to me. Listen.
THOU SHALL NOT FOLLOW)

Blood begins to trickle down your chin,
to your throat, down your chest,
as the metal tips of the machine
scrape against the bone.
The gates of the machine are built by doubt
to engineer your fears and your hate
and to make your questions hard
and deaf to any answer.
(Don't listen to me. Listen.
THOU SHALL NOT REASON AND COMPARE)

The machine pauses as it digs into the first layer of bone
deeper now, it clings, you feel
something begin to move
the sound of something acting
an action without life
like a Newtonian diagram.
A fissure opens, breaks, your skull shakes,
and something deeper than blood oozes out.
(Only those with an ear to hear:
THINE BUSINESS IS TO CREATE)

Give me your brain,
let me teach you to ask
as I taught Socrates,
soothes the machine
(Thou shall not doubt.)
Give me your soul,
for with it you blunder
and despoil
and with it gone
you are free from guilt.
(Thou shall not follow.)

Look at this,
and consider that,
and think on what I tell you
for you see
there is only one truth,
unite with me, the great eternal machine,
or fall as the dross of humanity.
(Thou shall not reason and compare.)

A single line of human thought
a great train
a bridge to anywhere

a tower to pierce the heavens
the fruit of gods
worship, devotion, fame.
You need only kneel and give your vision
to a greater vision,
the vision of the perfect
machine of man.
(Thine business is to create.)

Blood drips like rain from your feet
you quiver as pain dances your spine over
and the stately machine
squeezes you
with endless questions.
If you do not want your mind crushed
and devoured
then listen not to me.

Thou shall not doubt.

Enter Not

"In every voice, in every ban,
The mind-forg'd manacles I hear."—William Blake

Divided visions and marching ghosts
in a reality of shaking waves
no sea contains the multitudes
of drowning, breathless, stupefied
imaginations.

Write lines on a sheet of life
and hope they mean well
because your words spoken like
shattered raindrops piercing
can't be recalled.

A poem is a waiting game
listening for a friendly demon
or an angry angel
to smite you with a reprimand
of dancing music.

Patterns break universal chaos
they ruin the mechanics of science
and slice like blood opening
lifeless veins forcing
motion and thought.

Enter no machine. Enter no machine.
To hell with cordiality,
screw those spineless guilty fools
who think killing lambs
will save the earth.

Take off your manacles.

The Progression of the Metallic Species

Space Log: Entry 1

This will be my first task as Interplanar Research Technician. I grow anxious to reach the solar system I was assigned by the Alien Intelligence Committee. Though I have been on alien planets in the past, they were explored, thoroughly researched, and domesticated long before I was born. This planet is strange. We have visited it in the past, but until now no systematic attempt to contact or study its lifeforms have been made.

As with all initial planetary research missions, my task will be to learn if there is any significantly intelligent life, and ascertain which lifeforms are to be regarded as dominant, peaceful, hostile, etc.

According to the itinerary, I will be landing tomorrow. It will likely be a while before my next entry in the log, since I will be gathering masses of crude data as quickly and efficiently as possible. Once the data has been examined, I will report back.

Space Log: Entry 2

I have been on the planet for almost a week now. According to the committee's guidelines I have studied the largest bodies of the planet, since those planes will have enjoyed the most space for the mechanics of evolution to take place. Much like our home world, this planet is covered with large quantities of water. So it is the ocean depths which I explored first. Again like our world, the water is teeming with marine life of all sizes. Some are microscopic; others rival our largest space vessels. Such variety is quite promising for the planet as a whole.

Unfortunately, I detect no sign of sentience. Some of the beasts are intelligent in an animalistic sense, but possess none of the higher mental faculties of people: there is no sign of a developed linguistic system or other cultural indicators. I will continue my research underwater for a while more, but unless I find anything concerning the objective, I will not report anything more on the oceans.

Space Log: Entry 3

My research confirms at last another similarity to our planet. Life undoubtedly began in the oceans here and moved inland. It turns out that one intelligent lifeform does indeed live underwater, and this discovery lead me to realize that evolution has spawned on this planet an entire host of intelligent creatures.

These sea-dwelling lifeforms are nothing like people as we conceive them, but at length I discerned unmistakable intelligence in them. Their hides are made of a thick, glossy scale, and they are shaped rather like the trunks of large vegetation. They are capable of defending themselves by emitting some sort of discharge, perhaps waste, which is quite devastating. I thought they were mere animals until my equipment detected energy emissions similar to telepathy and other forms of communication used on other planets which do not rely upon sound waves. I call these the Sea Fathers, for it is my suspicion that these huge, magnificent creatures are the origins of the intelligent life elsewhere on the planet.

I thought this first discovery was interesting enough. Then I followed one creature to its lair. From its hide proceeded smaller creatures which initially I thought must be children of the beast. These creatures also showed signs of intelligence, but were obviously inferior and subservient to it. They tended to its needs, both for nutrition and hygiene. Their treatment of the beast was absolutely reverential.

I discovered at length that some of these creatures were slaves to a similar beast. These I will call the Surface Children. Surface Children are more diverse than their parent species, it seems, though they may simply have a many-staged growing process. Unlike the Sea Fathers, Surface Children are usually amphibious, taking roost on beaches at night or when tired. The smaller, softer creatures are always tending to them—if the Surface Children appear upset over the least thing, these creatures rush to appease them. The hierarchy is so blatantly one-sided, it is somewhat sad. Of course, our species cannot judge, for we have done similar things.

Incidentally, I apologize if I am not very good at descriptive language. My training as a scientist and intelligence surveyor keeps me from poetic expressions. However, I will do my best.

My going theory is that over time, the Surface Children began to move off the ocean, for many of them show signs of inadequacy at staying out to sea for very long. Evolution works wonders, I tell you! The most dominant species on the planet is in this group. I call them the Earthgrinders.

Earthgrinders have amazing adaptations for living inland. Instead of propelling themselves with their waste ducts, they are capable of gripping the ground with highly adhesive, elastic material, much like the feet of some climbing creatures. This flexible skin on their strange, circular feet allows them to blaze along at impossible speeds. They have also developed interesting ways of communicating. Their eyes are capable of emitting sequences of color fields, which indicate intentions, and when angry or excited can emit a high-pitched squeal of sorts. Adapted to be more independent, they have fewer slaves, but these creatures which I call the Devotionals are absolutely fervent to their devotion to the dominant species. But I digress. Let me first finish discussing the Earthgrinders; then I will look to their slaves.

Some Earthgrinders are quadrapeds, others are bipedal, while some have many appendages. They differ in size and color widely, and even within subspecies have endless idiosyncrasies. It would likely take many years to classify the entire species.

In the front of the Earthgrinders, I have located what must contain the brain and the heart. It produces great heat, much noise, and damage to the frontal region causes their vital functions to cease. The waste ducts which their ancestors used for underwater propulsion are now not crucial to movement, though they still emit cloud particles. Their food consists of many strange liquids, the contents of which I have not yet assessed fully. All the differences are hard to catalogue here. Their shells are still very hard, but have a variety of metallic colors and designs, the more vibrant and eloquent of which are quite breathtaking and likely utilized for mating rituals or social ranking.

Space Log: Entry 4

I had promised beforehand to discuss the Devotionals of the Earthgrinders. Interestingly, though the Earthgrinders require fewer slaves than the Sea Fathers, they dominate them much more rigorously on the individual level. Indeed, since the Devotionals are probably initially land creatures they are better able to escape into the wilderness. Some Earthgrinders, many in fact, lock their servants in cages every evening and stare at the prisons all night to ensure they do not escape. This, though, is seldom necessary. The Devotionals are often fanatic in their service to the Earthgrinders, pampering the beautiful, glossy skin of their masters daily.

Let me impress upon you the extent of the servitude ingrained in this poor species. They scarcely go anywhere they want to, but are forced to be trapped with the Earthgrinders on their senseless journies. The slaves are forced to feed them and assist them in every way, and are never permitted to travel far on their own. The Earthgrinders hate wilderness and oppress nature, destroying landscapes so they have more and more territory to dominate. The slaves are forced to create these dark, endless paths, creating more and more intricate patterns which slowly devour the planet's dry land and natural resources.

To encourage worship of the Earthgrinders, adult Devotionals give their children miniature idols of the beasts, inculcating respect for them at an early age. Festivals are held where they worship their masters, and great nurseries are devoted to the birth of the Earthgrinders, a process I must yet investigate further.

Evolution has taken a radical turn on this interesting planet. While it is intriguing, the servitude of the Devotionals saddens me. I know I am not to intervene or make contact at this stage, but I hope we can help the Earthgrinders to see the wrong they have imposed on the weaker class.

Space Log: Final Entry

I have been detected by the bipedal Devotionals, and must regrettably leave the planet for now, though I will return at another time. I will make one last report. I noticed another evolutionary step in the superior life=forms of the planet. These creatures force their Devotionals through rigorous physical torture, for they have divulged themselves of their own energy output organs. Now their Devotionals are forced to move them wherever they wish. They are evolved from the Earthgrinders, and still have two elastic, circular feet which grip the earth as with their contemporaries. However, two of those feet have developed so that they are elevated in the air, and the Devotionals must press their legs upon these flat protrusions to assist the haughty creature in moving. These Devotionals have named their masters, as I have overheard, "bicycles."

That is all I have for now. Further reports will be made when I arrive home.

Unodyssey

Countless scribes have told the stories
of heroes who struggled to return home,
but fewer have remembered
those of us who are unable to leave.
Traps are laid at every step.
Chores and family and no gas money
hold me at the door. And just when
I think I'm free
I think of what lies out there.

Street after street, senseless and deformed,
more potholes than cars, with lines too long
for coffee.
Erratic knights battle down their barbaric interstate,
roadkill bloodies their tires,
explanation in hand:
"Officer, my speedometer is broken!"
Half the way is riddled
with cone after cone after cone,
so the guy in the orange jacket says:
"Turn down ten blocks away."

Well, I've thought about it.
I think Homer can keep his boy.
I'll stay home on my unodyssey.

Merely Magnetic Explosions

northern lights
wave so cold
gazers left in wonder
relentless mystery

i know the answer
says the Man
its mere electricity
and explosions

but we who see
laugh and shake our heads
and say no science
demeans the mystery

Roadwork

An impossible task is set before me. I stare at it. It stares at me tauntingly, and I know I will fail if I try. What is the task? Good question. Explaining it is part of the problem. Let me see... No, no. I can't. I can't explain the task. Nothing I say will show you my anxiety or how hard it is. So I will have to talk about something else, something like it, and hopefully it might help you to understand.

I love to travel. I go to many places, several times a year, to help with the vexation. I won't bore you with the travel details. There's only one memory that stands out to me right now, anyway.

There was a sizeable stretch of wilderness between two cities, in a country I was visiting. Somewhere on the road, I came to two workers. One man was tearing up pieces of the road, the other laying down new pieces.

"Doing some patchwork?" I said as nearly as I could in their language.

"We're always fixing this road," said one man.

"Does it get used much?"

"No, not much."

"It gets damaged by weather or wildlife?" I asked.

"No," said the one doing repairs. "I have to keep repairing the road, because he keeps tearing it up."

"Well, why don't you tell him to stop?"

"He can't stop, of course."

"Why not?"

The other man set aside his pickaxe after extracting a good-sized slab. "If I ever stop breaking the road, then he will never fix it."

"So stop breaking the road and he won't have to."

"That's just it. He'll never fix it if I don't break it."

"But you're not getting anywhere. Roads are supposed to get you places. You don't tear up something good to fix it if it's not broken."

"Exactly," they both said at once, and went back to work.

Perplexed, I shook my head and walked away.

Graveyard of Good Intentions

So I went to the graveyard of good intentions
when I had a day off from work.
I hadn't been in a while and figured
a little atonement couldn't hurt.

I didn't recognize the voices
pouring form the tombs of broken hearts,
but I could feel the pain of lovers
who loved unreturned.

One ghost was a preacher
whose words he hoped would heal,
but when he lived no one listened
to his simple pleas for peace.

A cop shot dead by his own nephew
had thought to change the world
one troubled punk at a time.
"Scare him straight and he'll be fine, I thought."

A mother thought she'd raise some boys
and teach them to sing their hymns;
with tears in her eyes and the leather-bound
book in hand, she knew it was those good men
who were posted at the last bombing site.

I went to my grave and cried for them.
I promised myself to say the words I'd left silent.
Then I went home.
The next day, I went to work.

The Creature

"The excellence of every Art is its intensity."
—John Keats

A morbid weakness clung to my limbs and a shroud of dullness drifted about my senses. Like the hum of a sultry succubus, a buzzing filled my consciousness, spiraling around me so that the noise crept slowly between the shivering hairs of my skin and scattered my vision with obscure, snowy static. With effort I focused my energies and, though I could scarcely turn my head, I focused then on the vile summoner of that wretched sound.

How it made its sound puzzled me, for it was without the least movement. Indeed, so still was the abhorrent creature that it may have been dead or but a crafty semblance. But no, no it was alive and very real, for its primal rage, ugly and pervasive, soaked into me through the medium of its horrid, insectoid sounds. Its eyes were two misshapen, distorted mirrors, reflecting the yes and no, the salvation and damnation of every iota of light, dark, color and shape in those blackened, twisted, glasslike fields of perception.

Thin, sickly glistening membranes comprised the veined wings folded along its tar-like, loathsome body, resting over a plethora of tiny, barb-like hairs that covered its every part, including six crooked, deviously long legs that clung thirstily to the dresser-top. It stared and stared, and it buzzed, and horror and dread shook me as fiercely as my dulled members would allow. Surely the darkest sons of God alone could make such costume and don it in this world, a creeping mockery of beauty, the brilliant ebony of night become monstrous shadow at its hide and the cheery light of the morn twisted to shivery repulse on the bare reflection of its wings.

At the sensation of horror I attempted to harden my resolve, to fight the terror of the fiend guised as natural, poised on the corner of my furniture like a blasphemous gargoyle, having abandoned its perch atop some ecclesiastical edifice, only to come and terrorize with absurd, mindless revulsion. But as I fought that dread the Creature's rage grew, and with it the buzzing, and the noise and the broken shine of its infinite eyes climbed into my skull with invasive, inexorable voracity.

An alarm sounded, and I awoke, sweating. The dream soon left my rational capacity, but its presence and mood was not thoroughly banished. I shot off the fan and hit the alarm, looking at the time blinking up at me from the dresser-top. Quickly I gathered the things I would need for the day, then left my room, locking it and checking the handle before moving on. The interior of the house was quiet; the quiet of sleep, not of emptiness, for at the early hour of my awakening the other residents were still exhausted from the day prior. Along the parameters of routine I readied myself, and shortly thereafter departed.

The road I traveled in my daily life was unremarkable, with few turns, acres of trees on either side and a few houses now and again. I pedaled steadily, an even, relaxed but efficient pace which saw me to wherever I needed to go. My potential death rushed passed me only a few feet on the other side of a white line, the occasional vehicle growling a warning before mercifully passing on. I held the pedals still as I hurtled down a knoll, the rush of air refreshing and the sunlight racing through the branches to match and outdistance my stride. At the base of a hill my pace began to slow, and I strained my legs to continue at nearly the same rate.

Flies whisked among the tall grass beside me, buzzing the same buzz, the same drone they sang to the deceased saurian race. They cared not who heard or who watched; their only music never changed.

Passing a lawn I saw a tan terrier lazing on the grass. It lifted its wolfish skull at seeing me, and barking bolted from its place of rest to follow my path. The canine snapped its white teeth at the hem of my pantleg, but I pedaled harder and, amused, outdistanced it easily. Its steady barks slowly faded behind me.

With little more warning than the sudden appearance of a sidewalk, the countryside ended and the town rose up around me. There were more cars, their tires rolling with imparial commune on the asphalt, and other bikes, the click-clack of playing cards fluttering in metallic spokes, and old men gathered around a plastic table, outside a little restaurant, having the same sort of conversation one expects from old men in little towns.

By mistake I turned down one street too early. I thought little of it, designing to simply turn at the next intersection. But somehow I got lost, my wheels turning continually with my destination no clearer no matter how hard or fast I pedaled. An irrational fear then crept over my mind, and I began to go faster, my eyes wild and my fingers shaking. Suddenly a man was before me, and panicking I turned from him. The quickness of the maneuver threw my balance, and out of control I crashed into a fence.

Shaken, I stood and carefully extricated my bike from the crash. Looking up, I saw an old house, obviously abandoned. The door was open, the windows smashed, the lawn grown wild and unruly. Then I thought I saw a small, shadowy figure—like a child—dart inside, and it seemed I heard innocent laughter. Worried that someone had chosen so unsafe a playground, I followed inside at once.

The interior was as one would expect from the outside; derelict, in disrepair, with rotted floorboards, dust coated furniture and an army of cobwebs posted at every corner of the room. Again I thought I saw the shadow of a child, so I followed, insisting that the place was too dangerous for play. I saw a door shut, and coming up to it heard what sounded like giggling coming from the inside. Opening the door, the truth was then revealed to me.

It was not laughter but buzzing that I heard, and a swarm of flies burst upon my face as I opened the door. Confused and still convinced that a child was inside, I covered my nose and mouth and battled the creatures away, surging into the room.

I knew at once that there was no child here, for the room was too forthright to hide much of anything. Beneath the swarming flies, plastic bags lined the floor, each three to six feet long, similar in width, with the motionless proportions of objects that could be mistaken for little else. Delayed but no less powerful, an odor hit me then and I fought the urge to vomit. At once I turned to flee.

Something like a man, in height and pose, blocked my way, with dark, gemlike eyes and pale skin and a smile devoid of humanity.

"Flies are the sons of spiders, my child," he whispered.

I screamed and could not move.

In a classroom, or perhaps your house or on a lonely street, in the lazy heat of summer, should you feel the whisper of a wing touch your skin or the hum of flight grace your ear, recall my tale, and shiver at the broken souls who feed because they are consumed.

I Am Kafir...

I speak to you in the blood of spirits...

I slip so close, but you can't see me. Like the faintest whisper of a dead wind or the wisps of decaying cobwebs, you think you feel something as I brush pass, but you are not sure...

When the burning eye lowers, I prowl, a shadow, a predator, the formless power of your every nightmare...

I am alone. I have kindred, and we meet at times, fellow hunters among prey, but we are solitary, we are our own darkness, and we do not yearn for company like weak flesh. We brush beside one another, and continue on our lonely paths, surviving, eternal...

To be immortal, skinless, free... I have heard whispers of discontent, in passing, from my brethren. They wish to feel with fingers, to taste with tongues, but I laugh at such longings...

The trappings of mortality are so frail... Perhaps I was clothed in such weakness once, but I have transcended it, left it behind so long ago, that if it is there to be remembered, I do not wish to...

When Egypt was supreme, I was there; when Rome was a sprawling god, I was there, and I endure still, the same as then. Wiser, perhaps, stronger, certainly, and the greater my power, the less a part of humanity I am...

Humans... I pity you... Perhaps one day, if I find one among you who is worthy, I will share my freedom with you. What freedom, you ask? The darkest laughter echoes at your envy...

Legends of my kind were fashioned by the most ancient among us, twisted lies of the truth to keep our natures hidden... Some among us were vicious, inflicting torment among mortal flesh... But I see such sadism as urges entirely too human to engage in them, now that I am ancient and wise...

Who are we? We visit you when you sleep, when you start in the darkness... You cannot breathe, you cannot move, your heart beats with fear, for you sense what we are, though you do not really know...

My visit will leave you tired, perhaps, a little drained, but unharmed, so do not fret... You may struggle, but it will not matter... I will take from you what I need, and drift away...

Perhaps now you begin to perceive my nature... Perhaps you fear it... Perhaps, if your blood is strong, I can teach you freedom...

I Know freedom

Some say delete responsibility
in Webster's latest edition.
The children are all growing up
with no choice in mom or dad
and genes and science and God
and every puff of wind
puts us at Fate's whim.
For every act is caused
and freedom is a lie.
I tell you I don't like to rhyme;
the determinist knows why.

Well I don't know what Freud would say
about my psychology
or if Einstein would reduce my heart
to a basic line of theory.
But I know what freedom is.

Freedom is a little girl tucked
inside your arm,
and freedom is lost in love
and found in each real smile.
If you can't tell freedom when it's there
from when it's not, I can't teach you how.
But I've seen my sister dance and laugh
and I kiss her little cheek goodnight and think,
I know freedom when I see it.

The Cold, Hard Facts

On a warm, sunny day, Big Foot emerged from his cave, stretched, and walked into the forest. Before he got very far, a scientist wearing a white lab coat and holding a clipboard interrupted his ramble.

"Excuse me, Mr. Big Foot?"

He turned his dark, proto-human eyes to the man.

"Very sorry to interrupt your day, sir, but…"

Big Foot looked away and began to move on.

"Wait, Mr. Big Foot! I am here to inform you of something important!"

The missing link looked back, bored.

"Sir, I am here to report that you do not exist."

Big Foot stared for a moment, shrugged, and walked away.

Moons

Step into the sun and
feel the light on your skin.
Step onto the earth and
feel the warmth at your feet.
Step beneath their daughter
the moon.
Cradled by the earth
and lit by the sun,
we are moons.

I stood with a pen in my hand,
the ink dripped,
sank into the earth,
and became a world.

Let There Be Light

"Where man is not, nature is barren." —William Blake

I was once told to believe
that truth lay in textbooks and test tubes:
"A proper formula of rational insight
is like an undying lantern, and
should you follow its flawless rays,
you shall emerge, free, from the cave."

As if the trees and rivers know math,
or the owl and the mouse know their place
in necessity!
"Remember that there is no mind in the world,
that there is no idea without sense,
and without eyes, ears, or skin, nose or tongue,
we are divorced from truth.
We carry no lanterns, only windows,
and our house is unintelligible without the sun."

But the mind, says Blake, wields the senses
as a hand wields a hammer.
When they hoped to create a world without humanity,
they destroyed the thing itself. So I sang back:
"Truth is not given but made
by man and God, for there was no light
before words and eyes, and minds
to use them."

The Odes of Fancy

Ode of Fancy I: The Peril of Death

Masses of men
who walk the earth
fear their inevitable doom.
It is the curse of a mortal mind
to see its body's end
as the final destination.
Coldly entombed in that reaper
is the unrealized potential
of beautiful minds.
Had Hawthorne endured,
what further depths of the human soul
might he have excavated?
Or that fated Romantic,
his days cut short,
death ill sympathetic of unfulfilled Genius,
what further nightengales' singing
mighthe have harkened to?
Cruel and cold you are, death,
to strike mortality upon preachers of
the Maiden of Fancy, that highest Psyche,
when such light they bring to us.

Yet see this immortality:
The Maiden of Fancy survives even if
her champions do not!
A sword can merely take a life,
but a pen can birth generations.

Ode of Fancy II: The Peril of Reason

What have you done, Prometheus?
Into the hands of mortal man
you have given the burning wisdom of Reason!
Their hands are too soft
to hold the flames of industry,
to touch the sparks of their own fate.
Consumed to dust and ashes
natural beauty falls
and burns hotly the forest of souls
of cold, self-righteous intellectuals.
By fire man eats the earth,
defiles the freedoms
and beauties of his lost soul.
Old Thunderfists was too harsh on you,
Prometheus, but conede the point,
if what you have done came from pity,
as noble intentioned as you were, doomed god,
you did not see the coming travesty.
We see them too clearly now,
burning men press burning hands into
a world made miserable by your gift.
Well-intentioned thief of Olympus,
we concede that the crime was man's
and not yours, but had you been chained
before the flames of Reason were placed
into man's tiny mind, then perhaps
the Maiden of Blake would never have
been so horridly wronged.

Ah, Maiden of Fancy! Loved by that crafter
of poetic myths! We pray that Poet—
Prophet's prophecies of thine abstract Providence
will prevail, for only in thine lips
dwells the power to cool
the unchecked flames of Reason!
Dark consumer, child of an unwitting Prometheus,
you bring a new death to man.
But where can you reside, where can you hide?
The shining light of the
Maiden of Fancy bursts forth
and cuts through your darkest veils.

Ode of Fancy III: The Peril of Fancy

Blake did not know
when he envisioned his
Maiden of Fancy
that in her lovely, hazy hue of
greater realities
she had an ancient daughter as lovely to behold,
yet deceptive and wicked as
the cold fires of Reason.
This Dark Muse fair
breaths out mists of aporia
and lulls her transcendent lovers
to a world of Forms without Substance.
Lost in a maze, a maze of elaborate
constructions of sophisticated nothing,
the Dark Muse strips her lovers
of senses and of the balancing scales.
The resulting revelers and lamentors rejoice
or sigh in vanity, aimless and witless and clouded
by whimsy, their roads go wherever and their
words say whatever! And her lovers follow
her seductive laughter, as her wedge
of abstraction cuts them from the solid world.

Maiden of Fancy! Meet Prometheus, and share in his flames!
The haunted halls of which the
reluctant Romantic feared
will be absolved of their ghosts
by his flames of Reason.

Ode of Fancy IV: History of the Universe

'It is,' said Parmenides
for 'It is not' cannot be,
hence 'It is' must be so.
It was Formless, or rather
it was all. Forms, distinctionless
first to emerge from it
was she, the Maiden of Fancy
and smiling soon after emerged
holding her hand was the Mister of Is.
They were of two bodies and two minds,
but of one heart, the eternities
of imagination and reality.

Children divine were born to
Fancy and Is: And these are
known to men as lady Wisdom, huge Reason,
sharp Understanding, ancient Justice, and sundry virtues more.
Reason and Perception mingled with their
youngest brother pride, and these three
learned to love one another well
and grown so fused and mighty, said they:
'Forsooth! The mister of Is, holy is he:
Yet see how the Maiden of Fancy clings
so tight to him! This fancy, she brings
obscurity to our Father, and to us! Let us
cut her away like dross from gold!'
And Reason, Perception and pride
These Tyrants three struck hard upon
the eternities, and rendered apart with violence

the Maiden of Fancy and the Mister of Is.
Swollen and huge, Reason, Perception and Pride
became like one misshapen god,
and the Maiden of Fancy was cast to the void.
With her went Temperance, and Tolerance,
and Beauty, and Relief, and many other Children
of the Eternities.
And for too long those awful Tyrants ruled.

See? shrieks the sorrowful Maiden,
for my Mister weeps and mankind sighs.
And from her fled her strongest, yet most vile child,
the Dark Muse. Among the Tyrants
she lived: and hatred she had for her wicked brothers.
But if man groaned under those three gods
they sobbed or laughed joylessly under her,
for while she could flirt with Perception,
or toy with Pride for her own ends,
oh, loathed Reason did she! And so warred the Tyrants
with their sister, and mankind suffered,
and the Mister of Is bled
and the Maiden of Fancy could only weep.
And so It is,
and has been,
while the Tyrants reign.

Ode of Fancy V: The Maiden's Prophecy

Cease, disparities! demands the Maiden.
Unity, completion, wholeness I pray.
Reason! You see a flower and let
Perception speak of its number of petals,
the length of the stem
and the migration of its seeds.
Flowers go into your scrolls and your books
of learning! Ha! What a place for flowers!
Put the flowers in the ground!
Pride! Why puff you so? You are of the
Forms like any and do belong, yet hark!
You do wrong to Reason and to Percepion,
your brothers, for you let them see not their
errors. Flowers in books! Where do you put
your heart? Do the hues of the
burning chariot of morn, as they glance
so fair on the early sky, or does the surface
of the scintillating, wide sea speak to you
as matters of your books, or your hearts?
Disassemble these sights with your terms
no more. They are whole, they are fair,
and you will not see them without me!

The Maiden sobs, for her children forsook her,
but she dries her tears and says,
Shall you ever treat your mother so? Indeed no.
My place with him shall be restored.
Reason, Perception and Pride, my sons,
one day you will appreciate my gift

as surely as you embrace Prometheus!
What a thing you have done, but it shall be
set aright, for the Maiden will have her Mister,
and the doom of mankind will brighten
and the blood of my Mister will no longer drip
from his untended wounds; we eternities
shall again have balance.
Reason, Perception, Pride, harken to your wounded yet
untainted mother.

Your tyranny will have its end!

The Little Planet

By knife the orange is pierced
and the crust of the world opens
at my fingertips, revealing a
second world within.

Like a tiny living sun,
each golden slice of the mantel
is self contained,
but unified by the white veins
and filled with the flavor of simple truth.

The remains of the old world are thrown away;
it is now my own. Breakfast finished,
I put on my coat and step outside
to explore our little planet.

The Silent Farm

The road could have been any road
stretching out before me
leading to any darkened house,
any quiet place throughout all
of quiet time.
As it happens our lives put things in the places
we want them
but space is a fantasy
abolished by the dreaming moon.
I turned onto the driveway,
stones crackling under my tires,
watching the winding path up
to my unlit home.
My eye traced the curve of the
hill it sat upon, rolling like a
shoulder of the earth, the grass
of the fields always running to catch up
as the soil shifted slowly over
centuries, a restless nightmare causing
it to quiver for a moment,
a moment during which whole lives were lived
and haunted the dreams of the earth.
To the left of the house, behind my parked car
the tall blades of vegetation whipped back
and forth as I got out, their motions
the visible prologue of a night-long dance of
the sleepless wind, gushing like a
tireless lover over the quiet slopes,

invisible love unlit by the cold
but happy stars.
On the other side the trees thrashed in the dark,
creaking, creaking, rustling, whistling,
and I think that when I went inside they
drifted across the drive and down the gentle
slopes they took the winds in hand
and danced until they were weary,
then after the false dawn crept back to their
beds and sank their roots back into the earth,
sinking, creaking, sighing.
Three empty silos stand empty at the driveway's
entrance, birds roosting in their empty rafters, and it is
here that the dark things creep while the forest dances,
until they can return to their verdant sanctuary.
A barn, abandoned but for maybe some mice or
and old weary owl, sits alone on the field.
No trees or houses dance in its pen, its
fence strings of wires, their power dormant.
In my room I lay and I hear the things
moving, the night spirits reveling, and lonely darkness
contrasts with the eternal communion of the stars,
the fields and the woods.
The silence of the farm is a soothing music in the winds.

Esnesruof

It would not be unreasonable to assume that I am a sort of scientific explorer. While that is not entirely what I am, it is certainly what I have been. Unfortunately, my profession is such that the great majority of my experiences would be of little interest to the majority of people. Rarely is it that I am so graced with an experience I think fitting to share; thus I am excited to place before you one such moment in my relatively unremarkable career.

During my time in a certain, fairly developed but mostly disregarded part of the world, I came upon a country which I had never seen on any map or listed in any book. Should I happen to recall its name, I will let you know, so that you can visit it yourself. At any rate, let us call the place Esnesruof. During my time there I found the country to be very hospitable, very comfortable and most civilized. But after a certain period of confusion, I realized a most unusual feature of the inhabitants. My guess is that, since they are a relatively closed-in country, with few visitors and even fewer resident aliens, the strange genetic malfunction the vast majority of them shared could only become more and more impaired. This is how I at last realized the oddity.

One day, I was a guest at an official's home for breakfast. His servants were preparing eggs, bacon, toast and other morning goodies, and the delicious odor filled the room. Now, the people of Esnesruof do know English, and while they have their own tongue, they guard it fiercely and never, or rarely, speak it among outsiders. So, in my presence, they generally always spoke in English which, I might say, was always more perfect than that of the ruffians born into our language.

"My, my," I said, "that breakfast does smell good!"

The family looked at me, and my friend, the householder, said, "Now, praytell, you do not use insulting language at my table, honored guest?"

"Why, no, not at all," I smiled, perplexed. "To the contrary, I was complimenting the work of your cooks."

"Certainly, that is much appreciated, but you *do* know that this word, this 'smell,' is entirely imaginary and has no manifestation in reality whatsoever?" he pressed, somewhat indignant.

More surprised than affronted, I put up my hands and said in a placating tone, "Sir, I know not what the word may indicate here in Esnesruof, but in America it merely means the faculty of sense located in the nose, which allows one to detect the odors of certain objects."

"Enough! I had thought you a guest of more propriety than to countenance these lies before my family. With all due respect, I must ask you to take your leave for today until I can settle the ridiculous questions you have raised in the minds of my poor children."

Accepting his further apologies graciously, I did take my leave, and quickly.

The incident left me in a state of distraction for the remainder of the day. I could not fathom what about my remarks had upset my friend so thoroughly. I had other appointments, and kept them, and by the following morning had shrugged off the strange event of the day before, supposing it some cultural idiosyncrasy of Esnesruof. In fact, I would have forgotten it altogether, except that in glancing through one of their science textbooks I discovered the following passage:

All knowledge comes from our sensual experience of the world. It may be prudent or virtuous to believe in things not experienced, but scientifically we must admit only the knowledge we can demonstrate sensually: namely, through our vision, our hearing, our taste, and our touch. These four powers are the only window into the mind of the outside world.

Perplexed and incredulous, I could not fathom why they had left out the sense of smell. After all, many creatures, such as canines, survive on that very power. In most scientific endeavors, that sense was usually not so important, but then neither was taste, generally speaking. How could they seriously exclude the fifth sense?

At once, I began to search the books in my private quarters. In none of them were kept words such as "smell," "odor," "perfume," or anything related to that function of the olfactory. In a passage on the nose I read:

"This body part is used to bring oxygen into the lungs. It possesses certain features which blockade the invasion of germs."

Frustrated, I threw the book aside and left my quarters, heading to the public library. I found the librarian that moment at her desk, reading a book entitled *David Empirice* on the *Elucidations of John Locke*. She noticed me, and set the book down. With a smile, she asked me what I needed.

"I am looking for anything related to smells," I said.

"Snails? Disgusting, but interesting creatures. Over in animology..."

"No, no," I said, and enunciated more clearly, "*Smells*. The perception of the nose which discovers *odor*."

Her face grew still, as one insulted, the look a smart child gets when he's been told to be good or the boogeyman will come for him. "Sir, we both know no such book exists. Please, don't upset people here by asking for such nonsense."

I stared at her for a moment, waiting for her to laugh and show she was jesting. But no laughter came, no flicker of amusement. She even appeared a little angry. Sighing, I turned and left.

I made my way to Michael Empirice. He is no relation to David Empirice that I know of; it is simply a common surname in Esnesruof. No philosopher like the man who shared his name, Michael was a foremost scientist of great severity and seriousness, and I knew his help would be useful in getting to the bottom of this most unusual affair.

He welcomed me into his home with his usual amiability. We spoke idly on various matters, him asking me about my experiences and stay at Esnesruof, and I inquiring after his business and research. At length, I broke into the topic which had prompted my visit.

"My friend, I have come to you inquiring after a certain scientific anomaly I have noticed among your people. As you know, I have been something of a scientist in my field, and so take interest in such things. I have noticed that your people make no mention of the sense of smell, neither in your textbooks or in daily life. In fact, a friend of mine, a mutual colleague, grew upset with me for mentioning the word 'smell' in his household. Surely, you can explain this strange phenomenon to me."

Michael sighed and rubbed his hand through his hair and gave me a sad smile. "My friend, I have encountered this issue among visitors before. I do not wish to hamper our relationship, but surely, you must know as well as I that this 'smell' is a fabrication, a lie and a myth of primitive cultures used to explain occurrences in the world."

I blanched. I had not expected this from my esteemed colleague. I thought perhaps he might be reasoned with; surely he had heard my case with more civility than others in the city.

"But there is plenty of proof, my friend. There are animals which move their noses in the air, sniffing and behaving according to what they sense. There is overwhelming evidence in terms of human testimony, and brainwaves activated as shown by monitoring computers when animals with this perception partake of odors. I myself have experienced them; I do so even now."

Michael smiled. "As to your notion of animals and brainwaves, I have a simple answer. It is called the Smells of the Gaps argument. Scientists have been unable in your community to explain the behavior of certain animals in conjunction with their nostrils, and so whenever they cannot fathom their behavior, they result to this ingrained cultural lie and say, ah ha! They have this sense of smell! As to your supposed personal experience of odors, well, that can easily be accounted for. Certainly it is in your feeling that you have sensed smells, simply because you have believed throughout your life that you can do so. You have, one might say, projected this belief right into your nose, so that you actually have fooled yourself into this illusory sense experience."

"Surely," I said with a laugh and a start, "you cannot think this so! The vast array of senses that *I know I have experienced*, with their incredible idiosyncrasies, could not be fabricated by my mind alone. Flowers, food, clothes, people, animals! Nearly everything, the wind itself tells me that this sense of smell really *does* exist. There is too much qualitative evidence for me to disregard, and surely you must credit me with my sanity."

Michael smiled and sat back. "Look, friend, I will concede your point if you can do but one thing for me. Describe a sense of smell to me so that I would know it, if I had never sensed it. If you can do this, so that its descriptive quality is so overwhelming I cannot ignore it, I will agree."

I smirked, confident that I could do this with no problem. "Well, that is quite easy. A flower, for example, has a perfumy odor, a light fragrance that is pleasant to the nose."

"Ah, and there it is, that Smell of the Gaps I foretold. A "perfumy odor," a "light fragrance," "pleasant to the nose." You cannot describe this smell to me without referring to it. A castle built in the air, I am afraid," he said gently, as to someone deranged.

"I… But wait. I can say this of the sense of smell. Some of it is more overpowering, like a very bright light, or very gentle, like a barely detectable taste. Some of it is enjoyable, some of it disagreeable. Surely these words are not rooted in odor."

"Ah, but you see, in this too you have erred. You have but projected your experience of your other senses into this imaginary one. Indeed, to describe it you needed to refer to the real senses, sight and taste namely. There is simply no means by which you can describe it to me in terms that I would know it, and as I have never experienced it, I have no reason to believe in this strange, pervasive cultural lie that has so deeply affected you. I am very sorry."

I was so baffled by this, I stammered for many moments, unsure of what else to say. Apologizing, I then departed his house and Esnesruof, struck by the pleasing purity of the air's odors. I knew, I *knew*, I could detect these odors. But somehow, a whole country had either convinced itself it could not, or had somehow lost its ability to smell altogether. I have not since returned, though I do plan to do so after my nerves about these things have settled somewhat.

Moonwatchers

I think I was dreaming that night
when I stopped to look at the moon.
My reflections while awake turn to it
so often, I can't be sure.
My eyes could not turn away,
I stood in a grassy field
in a posture of obeisance.

Dark clouds swept in wrathfully,
the yellow moonlight stood brave.
The shadowy forms became like smoky hands,
with long, skeletal fingers, eating at the moonlight.
The two hands closed in fiercely
but she would not be taken.
Moonlight flashed, and the hands recoiled, seared.

Again the moon turned in its place,
stoic, implacable, unafraid
as horrid and ghoulish the black hands
hissed like unbelieving demons
ready to kill the light of evening truth.
I realized I was not alone,
for other moonwatchers knelt trembling in the field.

The hands could not win, for the moon
was too strong.
They shrieked and struck the air like bats
and from their thunderclap
demonic hordes of shadows who

ignored their makers and the moon
swept voraciously to the field
with smoky teeth and claws they came.

Some moonwatchers fled, and she flickered.
And some turned to fight the children
of the dark clouds, enraged and set
to defend their moon, and themselves.
And each who fought died, and with every
gaze departed, the night maiden faded
and the dark hands encroached.
And they mustered their hatred and they
choked the moon and smothered her light.

Many moonwatchers let their gaze falter, and the
hordes devoured them. The field plunged
to darkness. A few of us, though, did not
faulter. Our eyes fixed on the black tumult,
the chaotic, mephitic shadows, and waited
unshakably. And moonlight clung faint
but real, like armor, to our garments.

And the hordes consumed everyone
whose eyes were closed or averted.
But they could not touch us, and when
their terror could not reach the faithful
their rage turned inward
and they ripped their own host asunder.
Then, darkness and still enveloped all.

Like the smile of an old lover long
away after a journey of great peril,
the moonlight exploded through the
shadowed clouds and the field
saw her light. And we, the moonwatchers,
cheered. The hands of darkness fled
and out crept the stars.

Mirror

The floor at my feet
is warm in the sunlight.
I stand looking out
from the kitchen window.
The circle of backyards surround
a public grass-fringed pond.

Its glass surface is perfectly still,
and in it the hazy blue and gold hues
of the early spring sky,
and the white siding and black roof tiles
of every house reflect perfectly
in its calm waters.

"I can look at nothing for very long,
except the sea," whispers King Haggard,
and Ishmael smiles knowingly.
I think there is indeed something to it.
Whether it's unicorns or freedom
or the urge to go a-whaling,
we are called by the waves.

A bird swoops past and its
feathers stir the water, the reflections
breaking in a ripple that grows from small,
until its tremors resonate across the pond's
entire surface. For a moment the whole
world shimmers and shivers.
The ripples fade, and the waves go still.